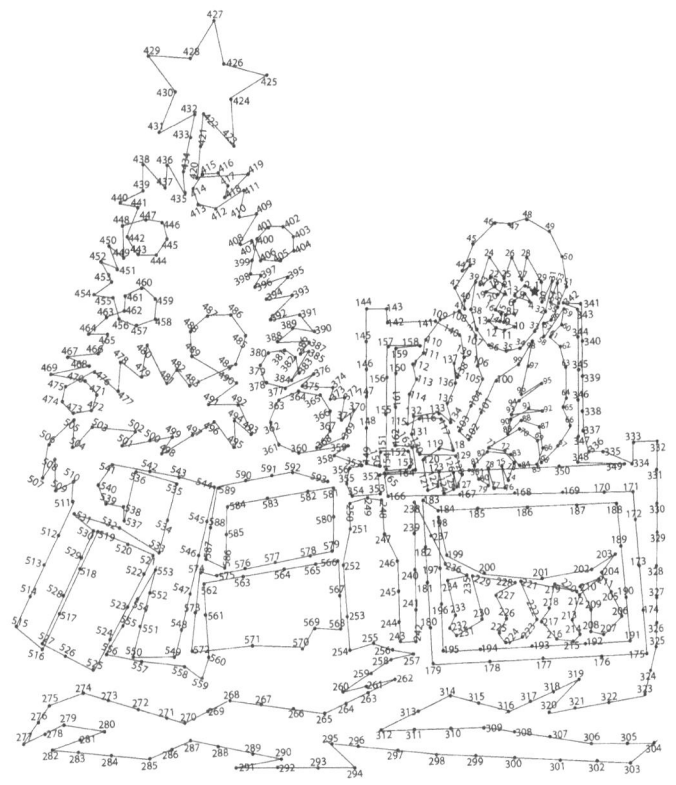

Christmas Dot-to-Dot for Adults

Dot-to-Dot Puzzles from 410 to 705 Dots

By Dottie's Crazy Dot-to-Dots

WELCOME!

We invite you to relax with the beautiful images

found in these pages whether this is your first

or 100th dot to dot book.

The directions are simple: Start with dot #1,

and draw a line to dot #2, then a line from dot #2

to dot #3, and so on. A picture will appear

as you connect the dots.

Take all the time you need and don't worry,

you will always find the next dot,

even if you don't see it at first.

We hope you enjoy this

super challenging dot to dot book.

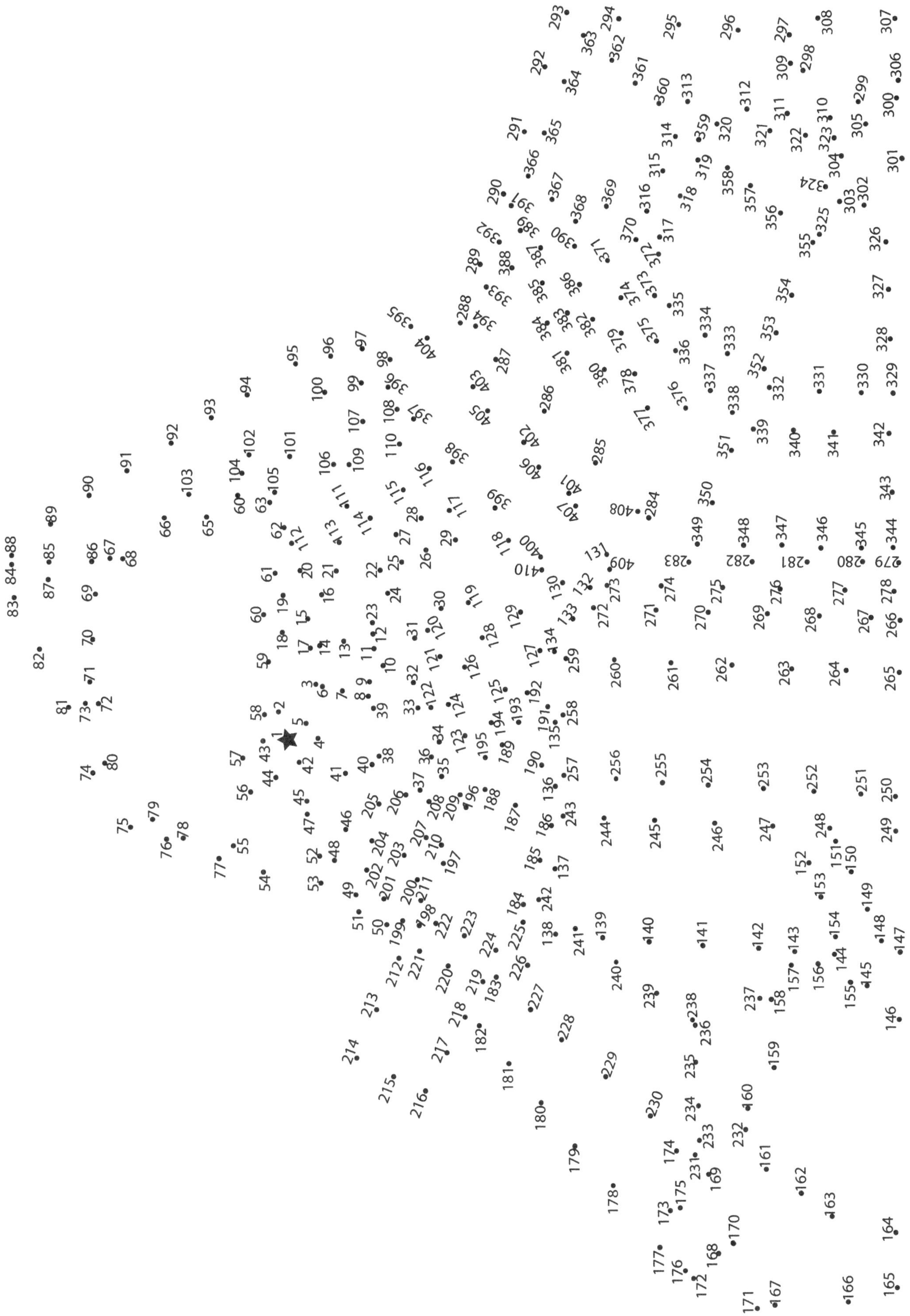

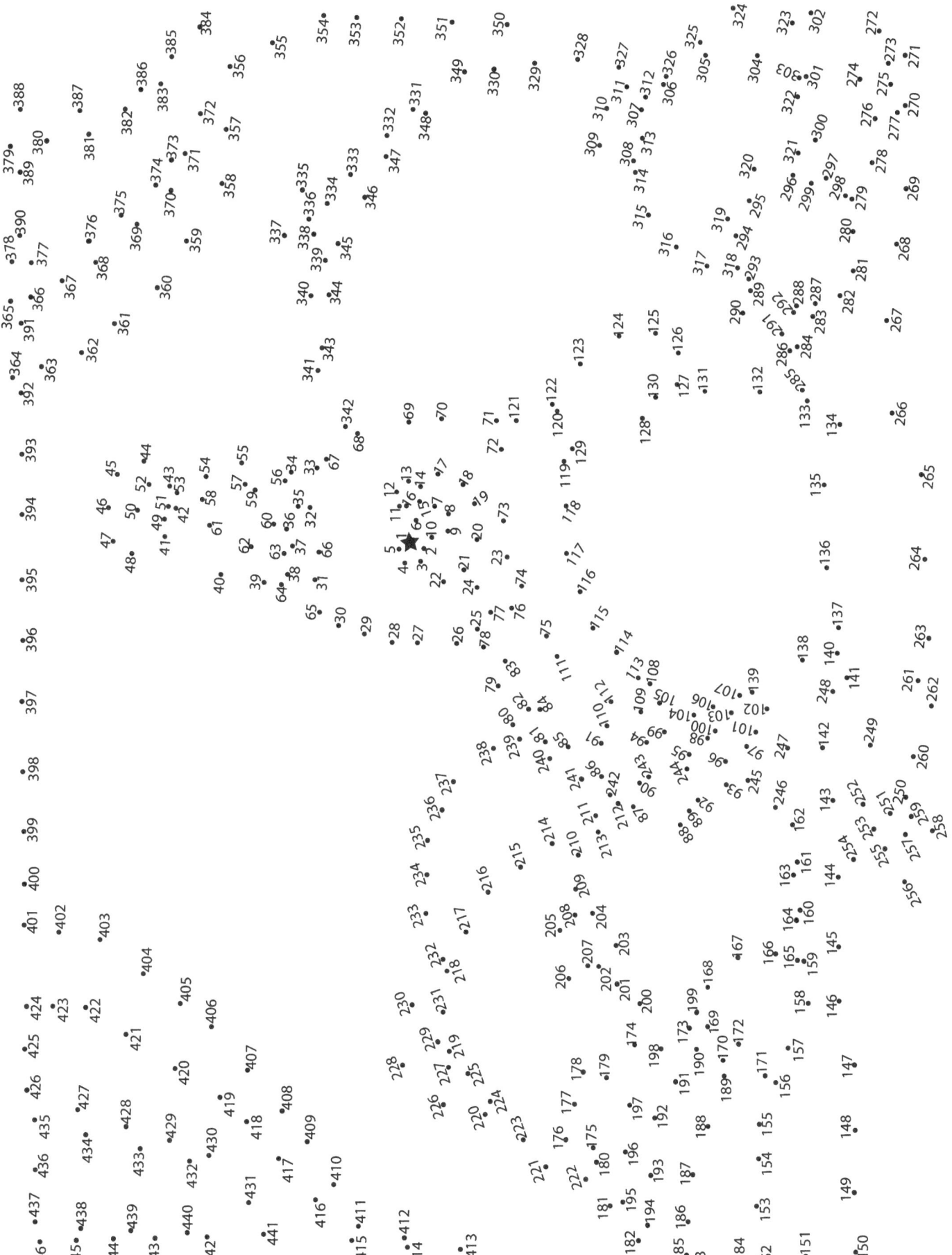

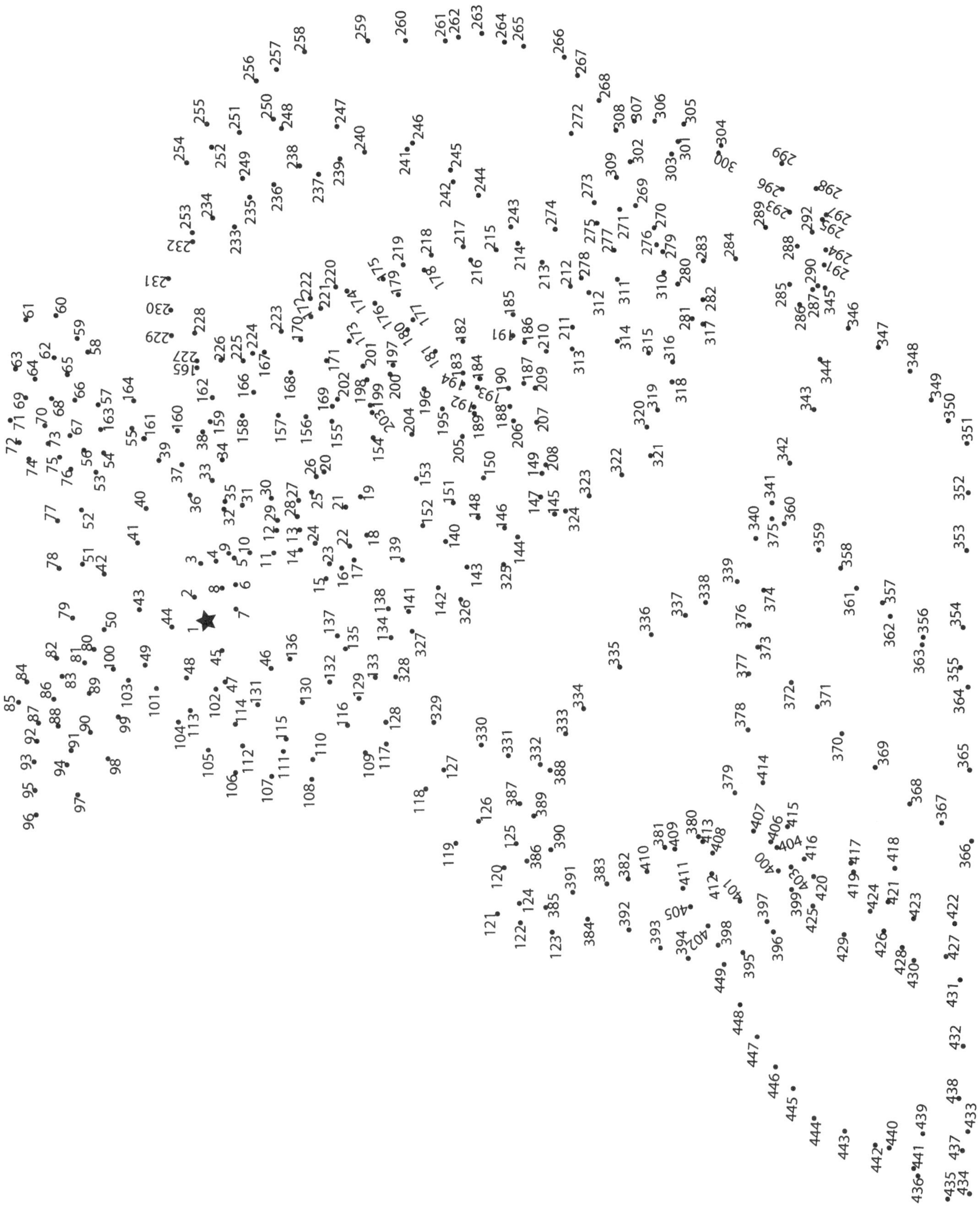

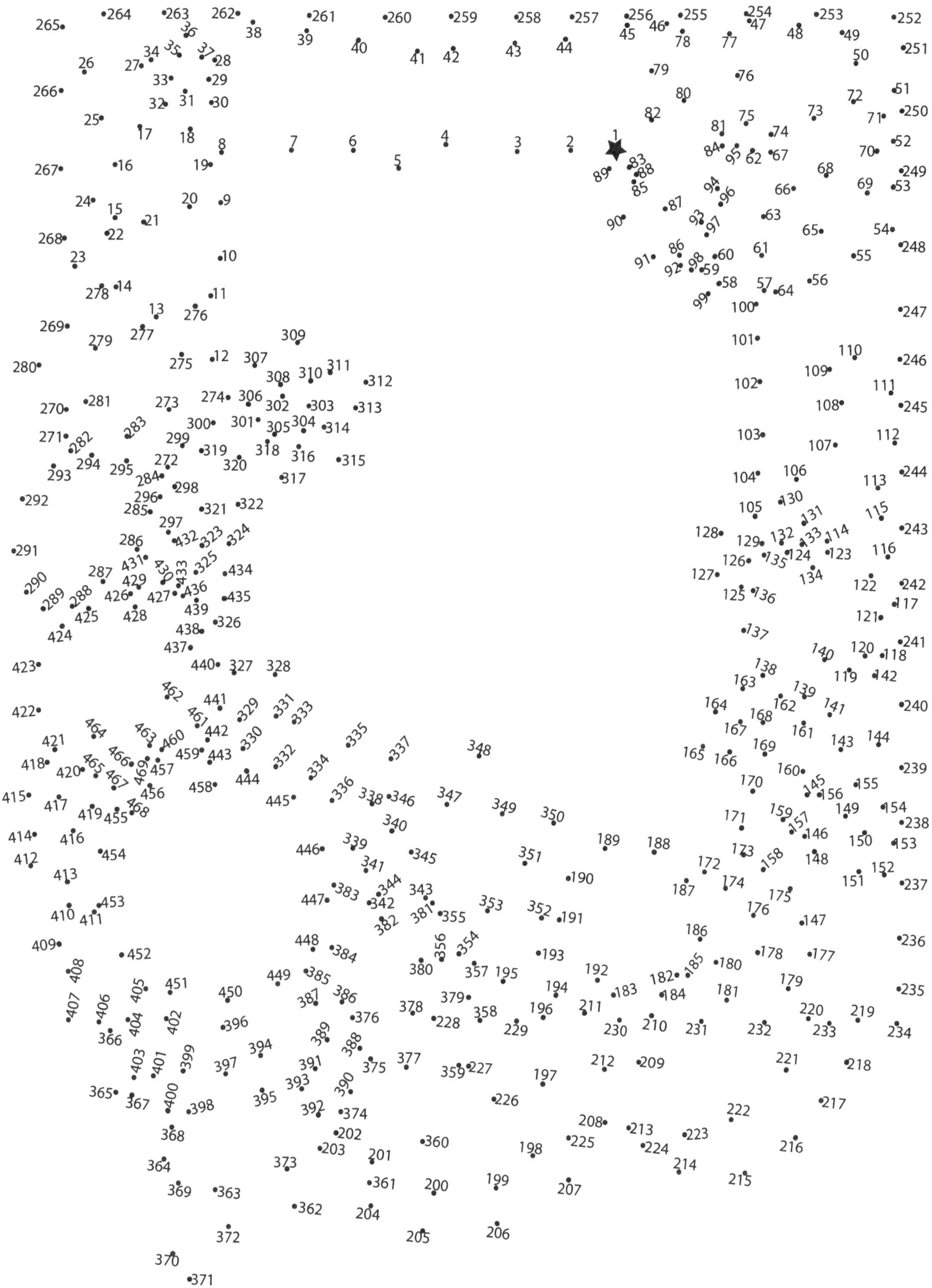

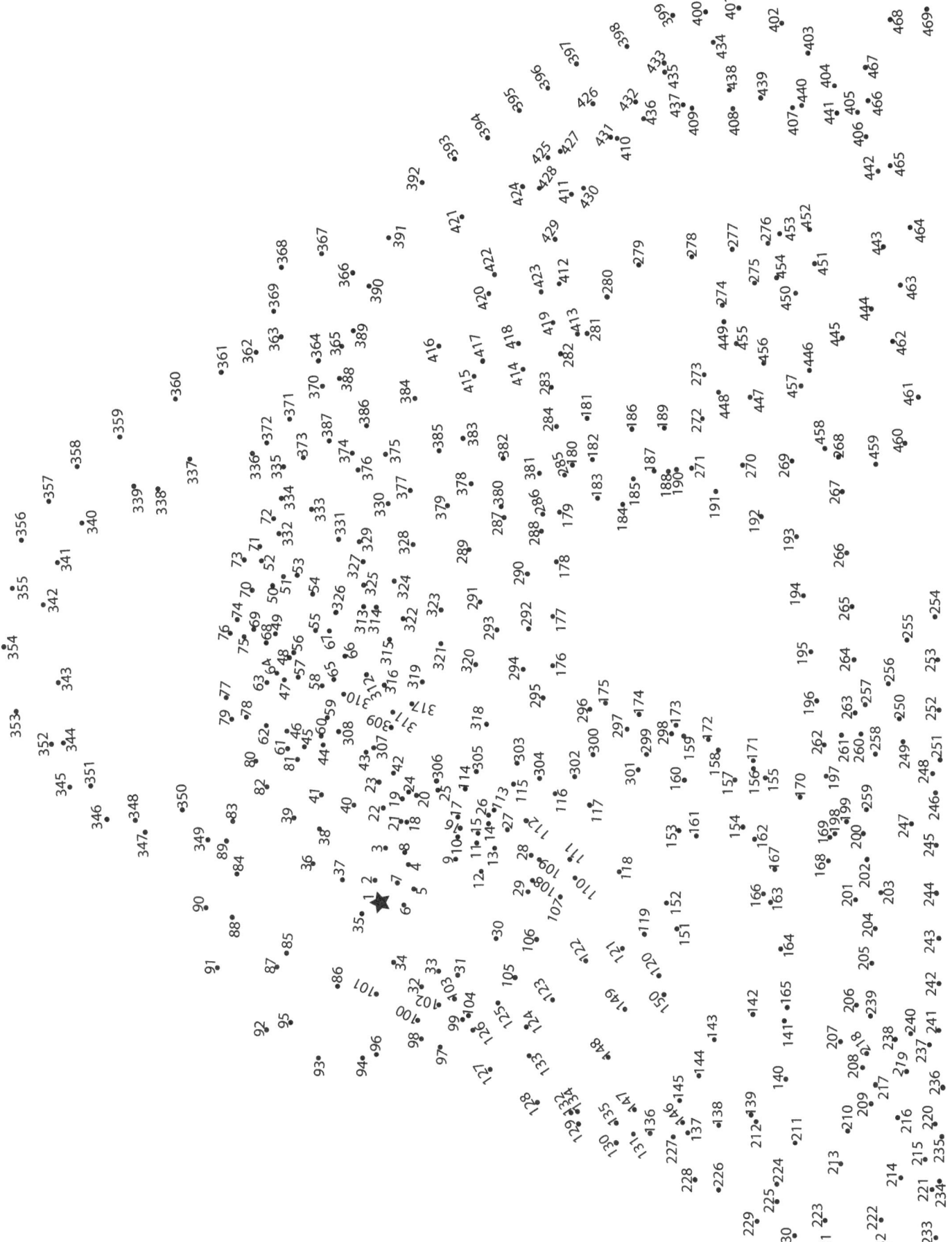

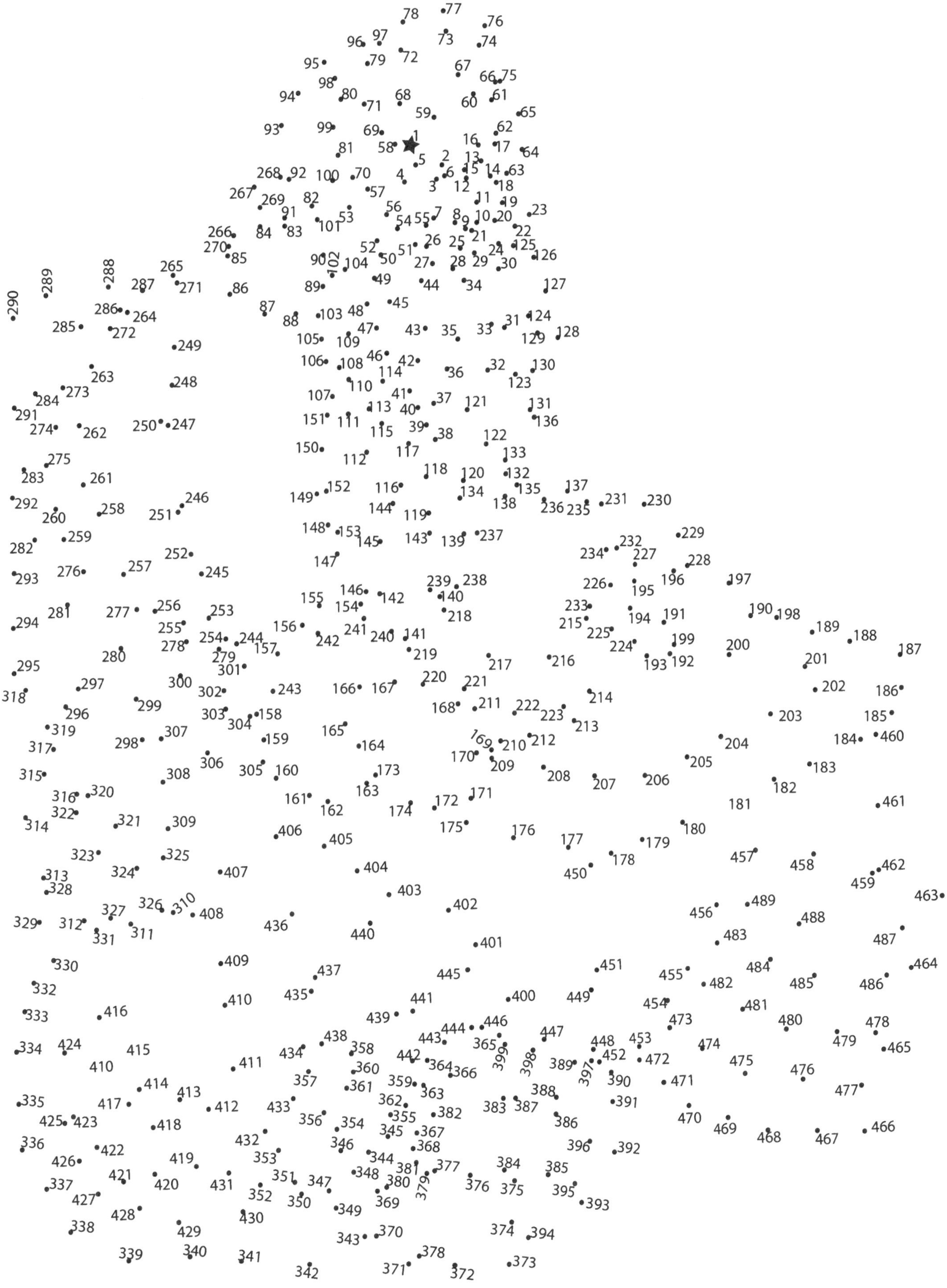

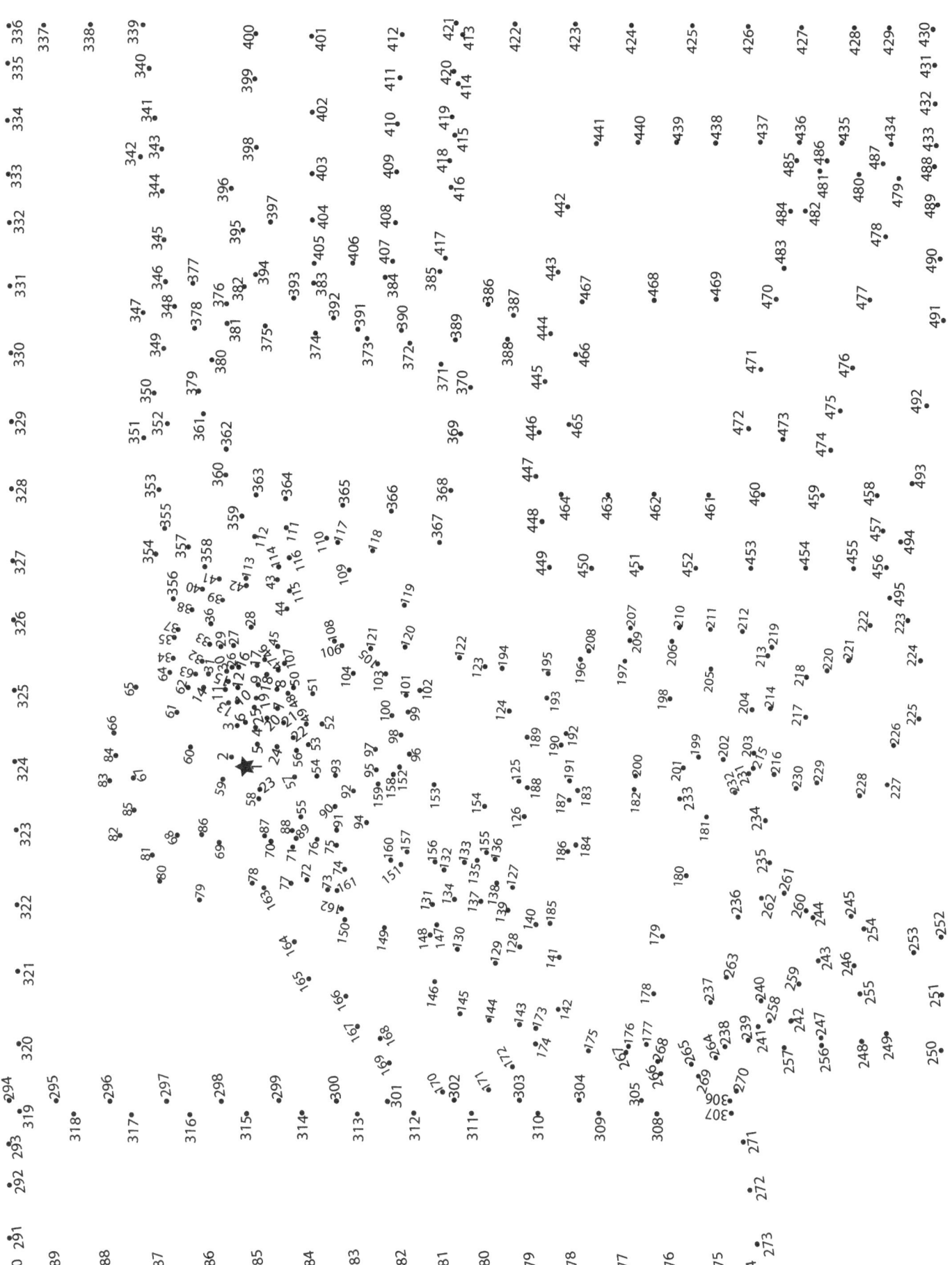

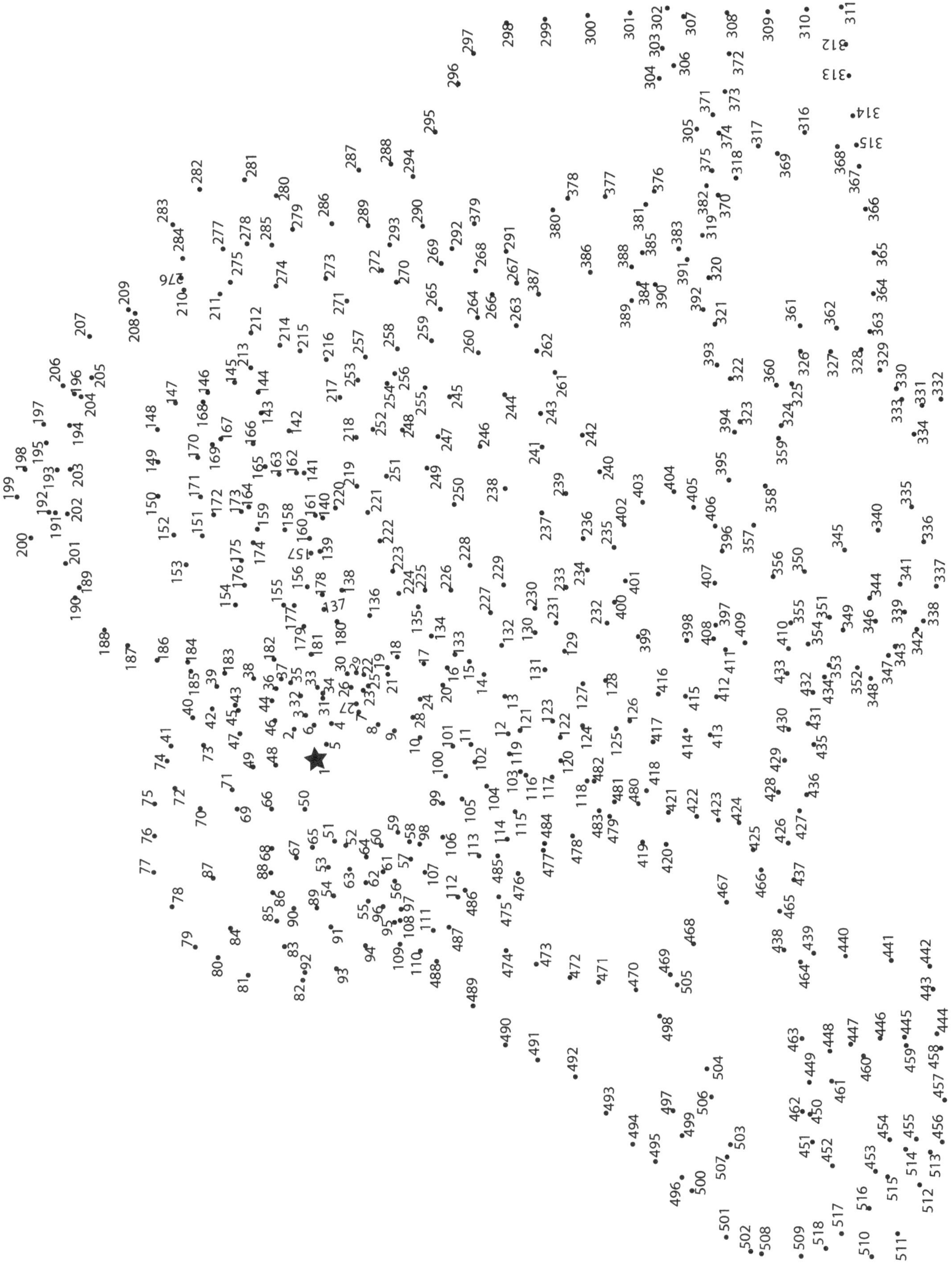

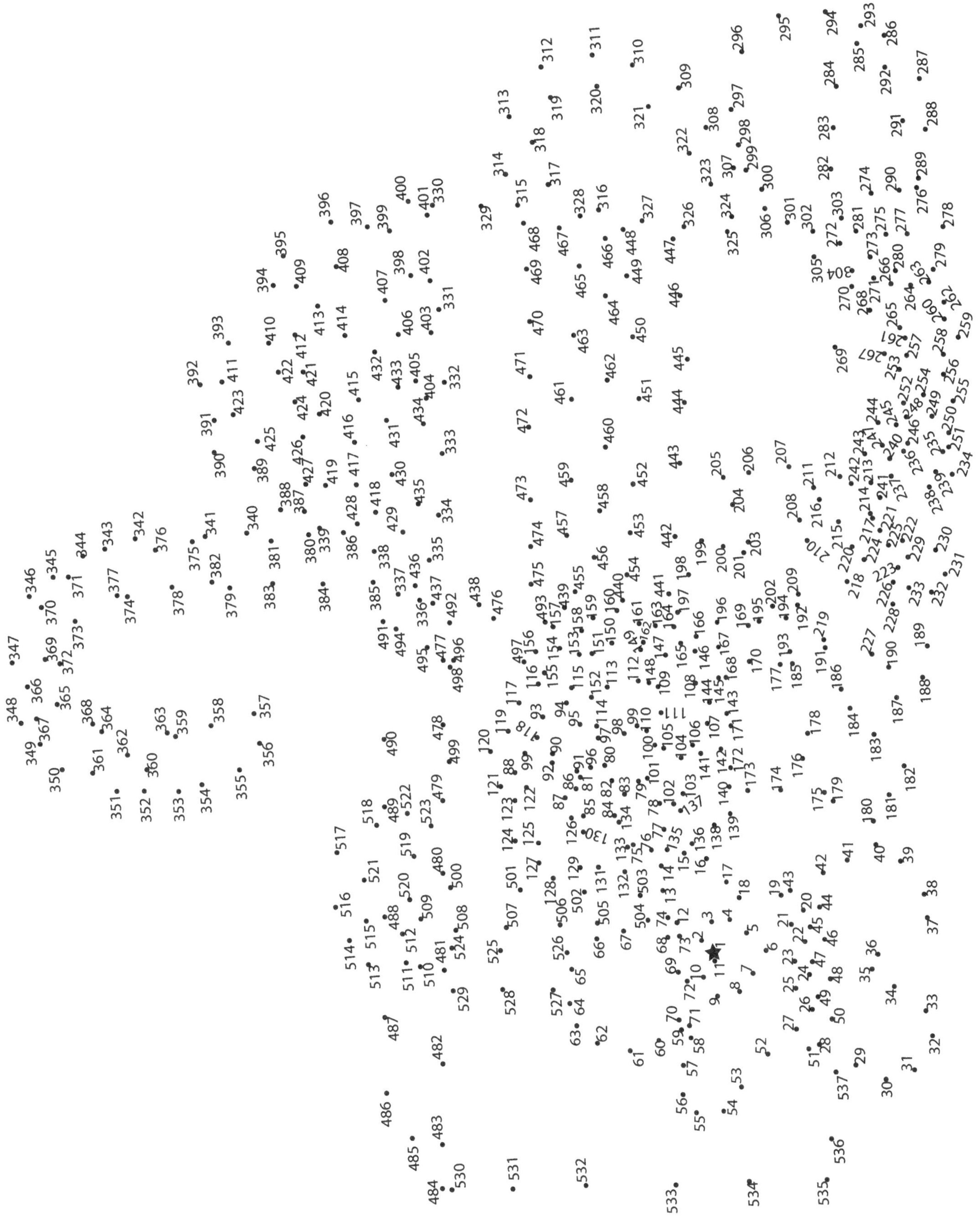

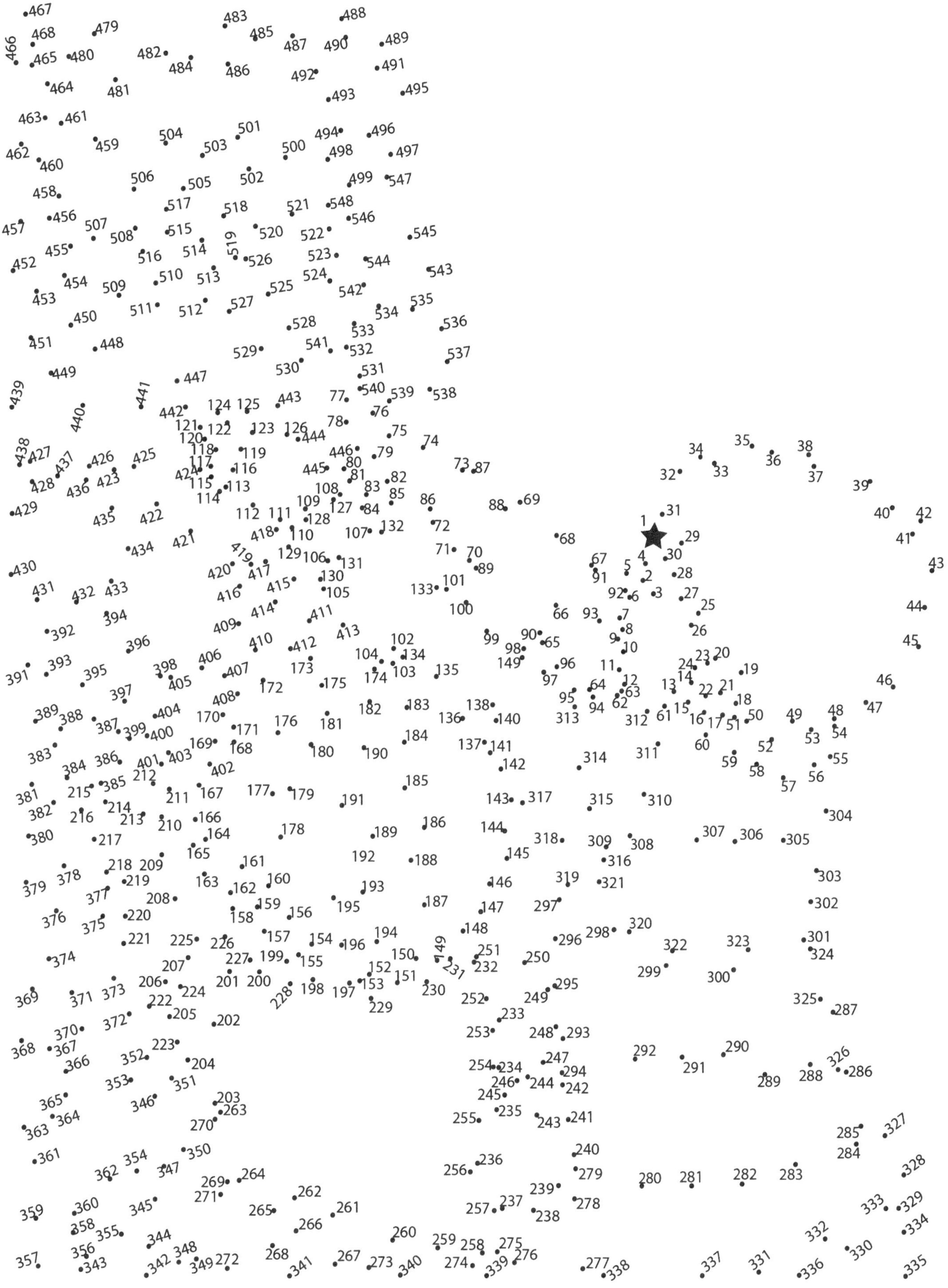

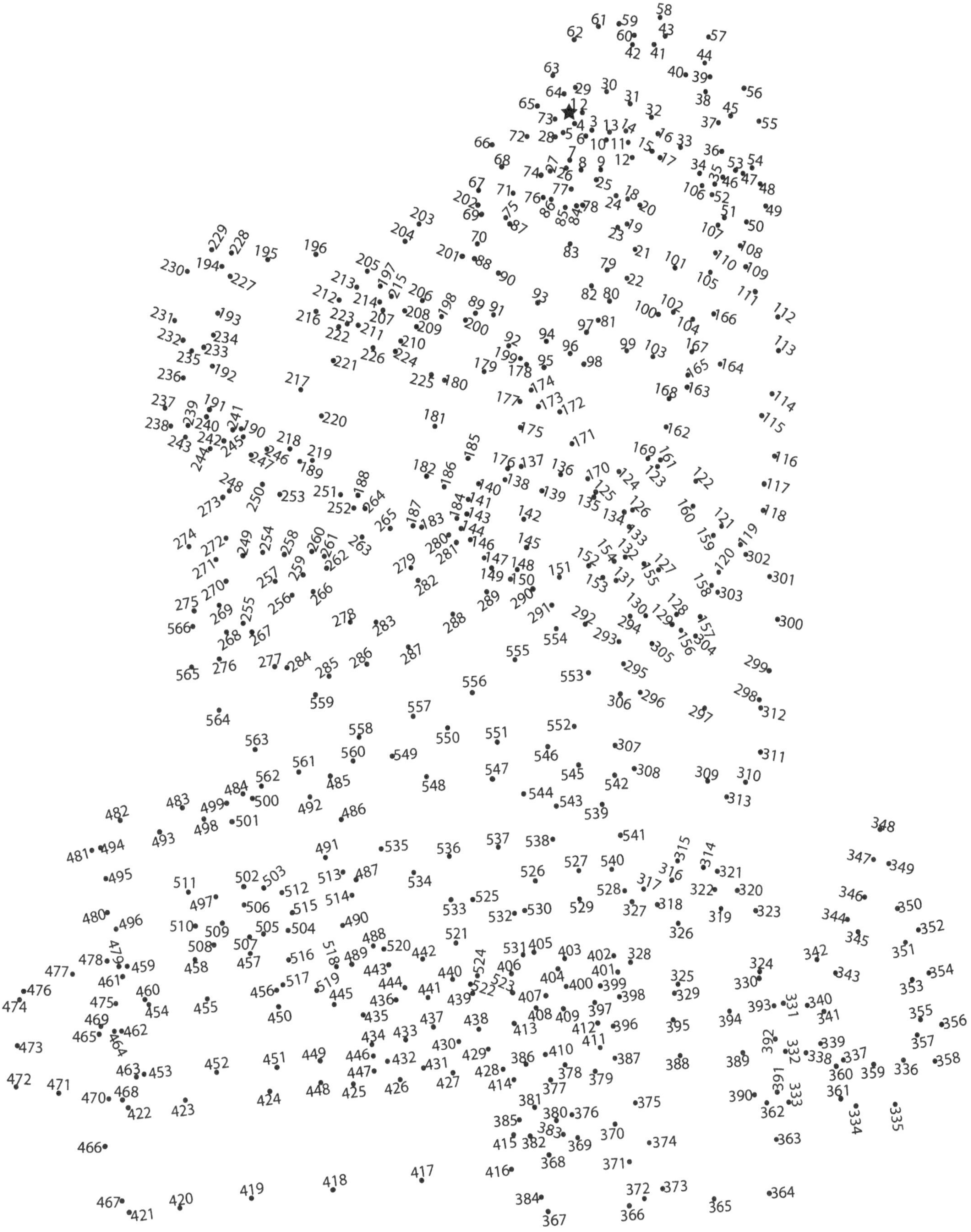

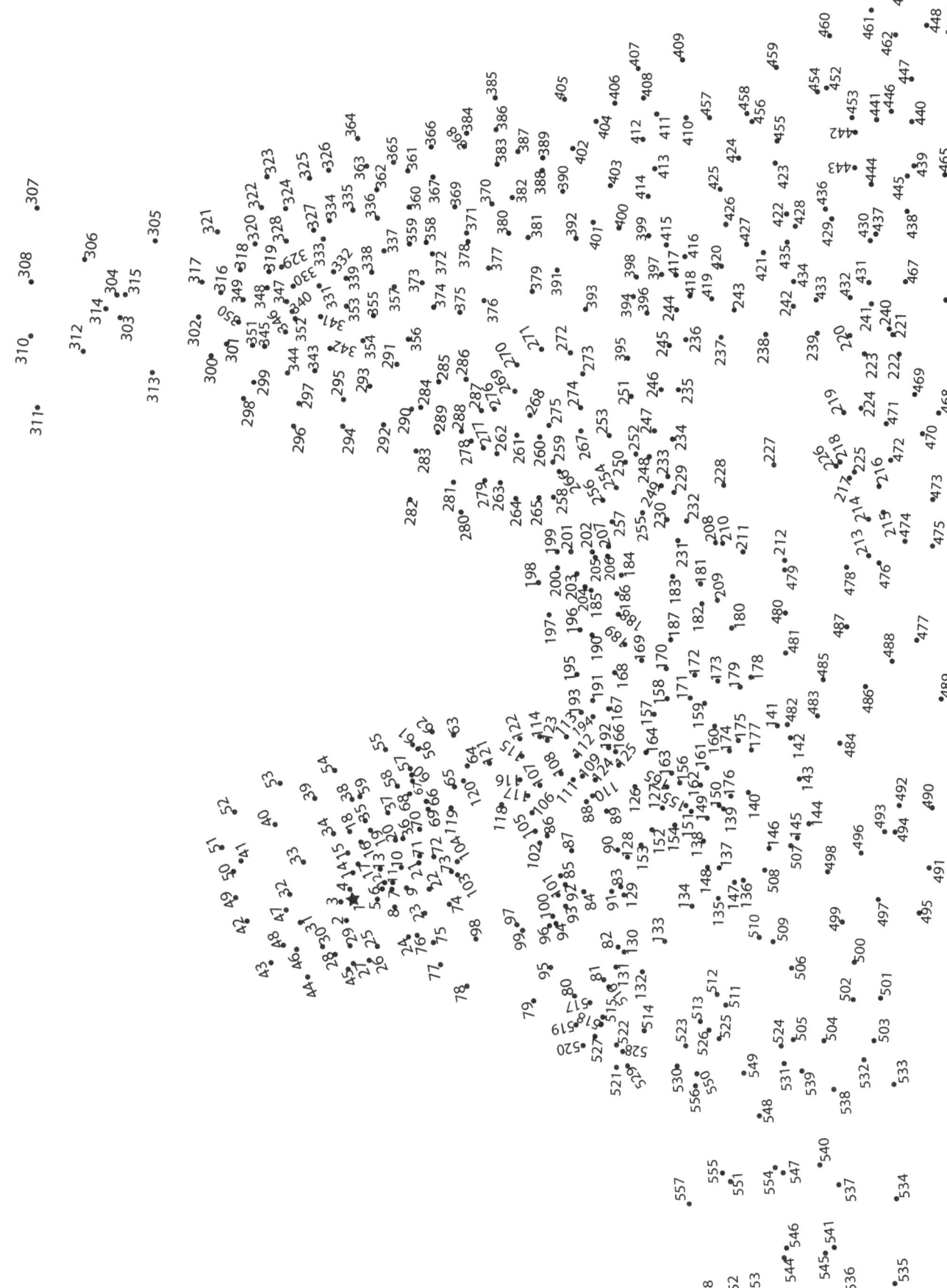

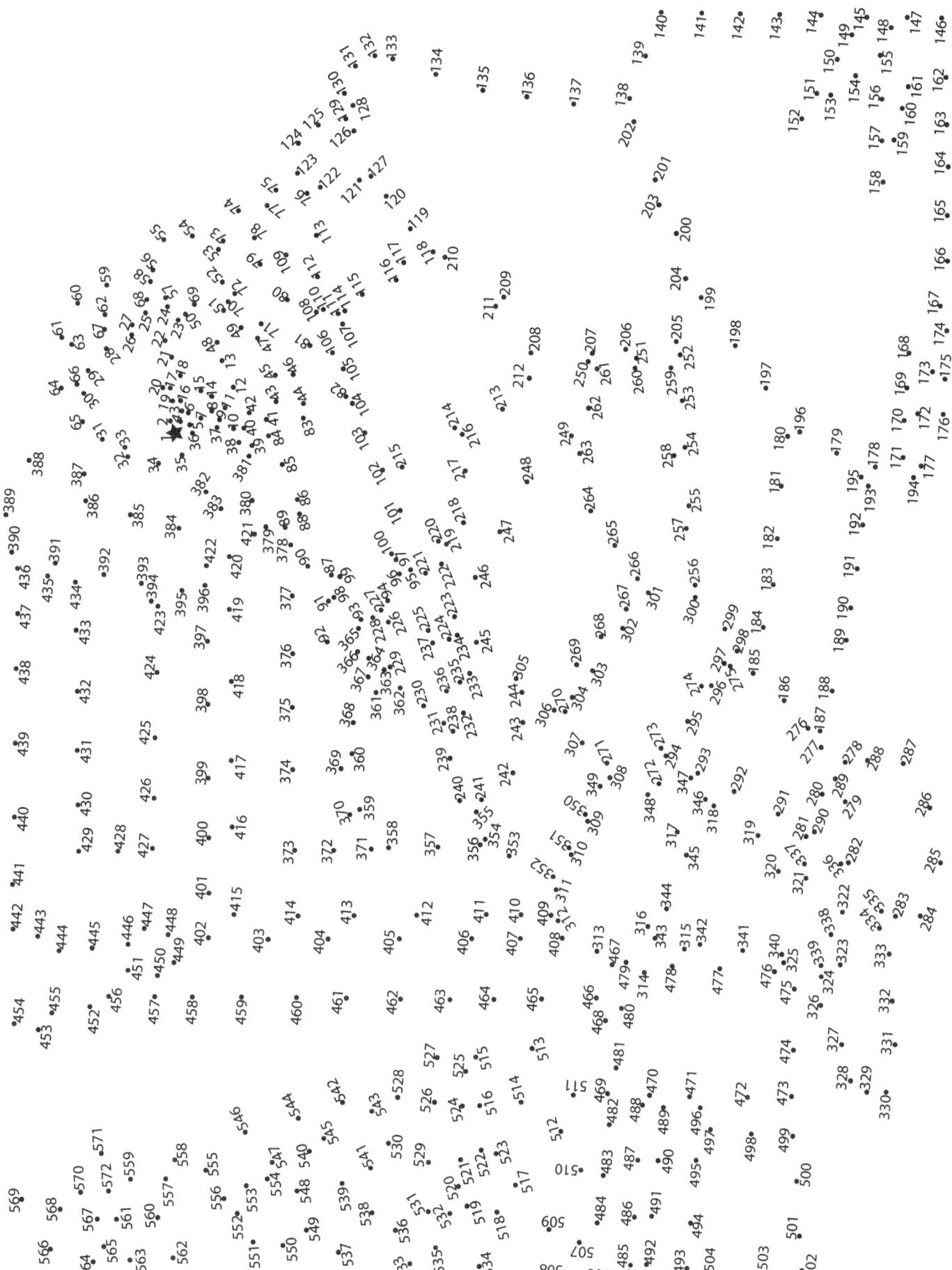

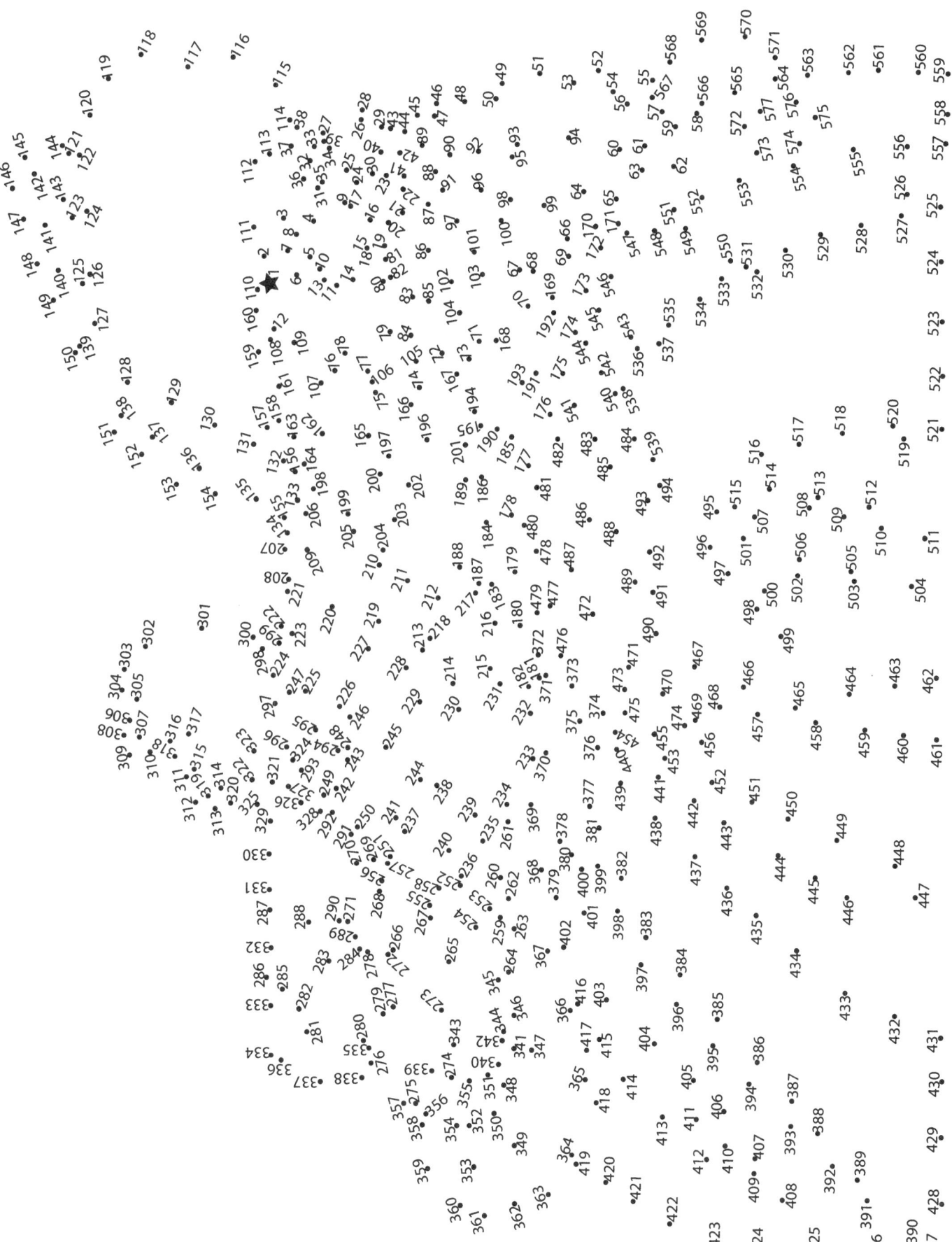

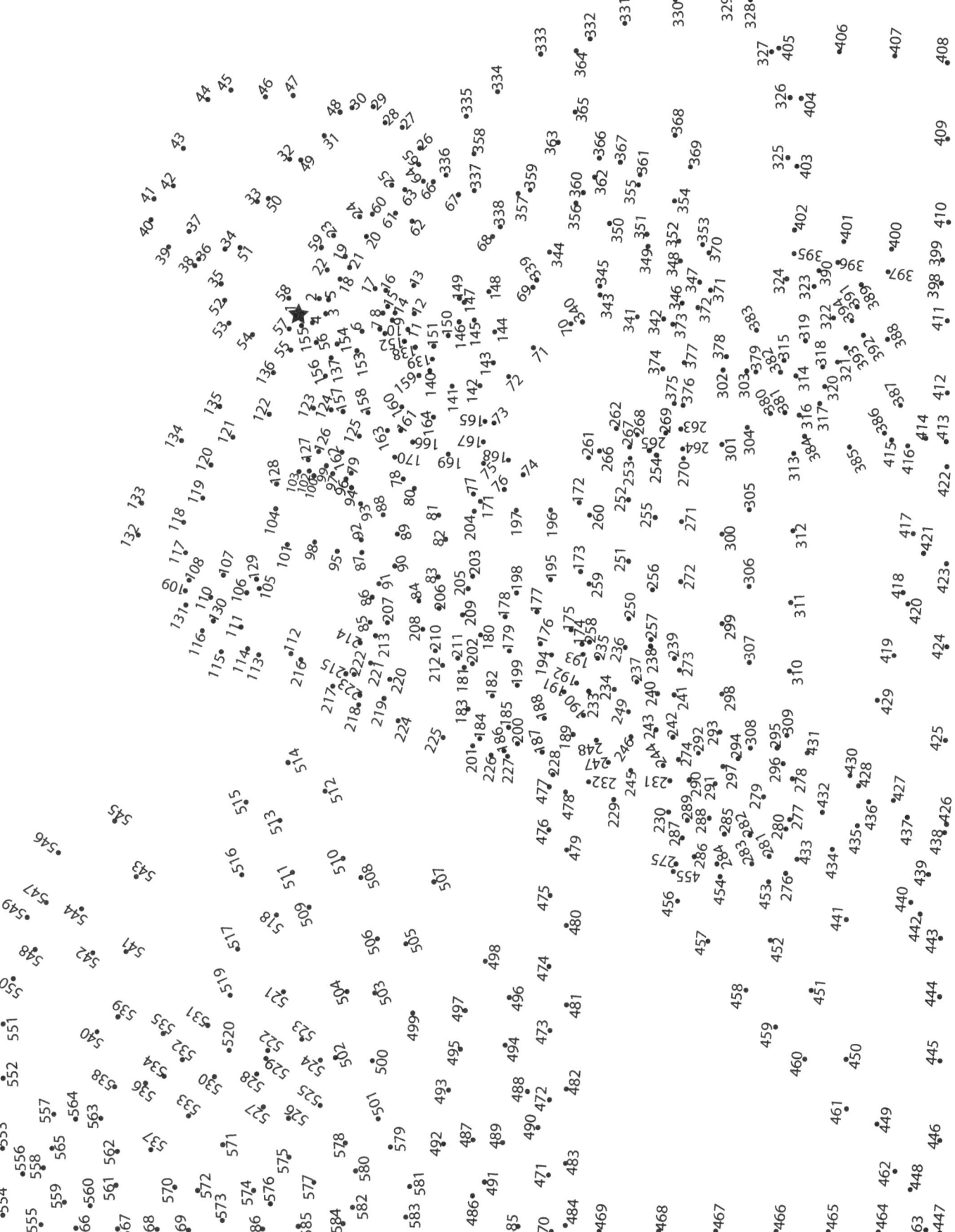

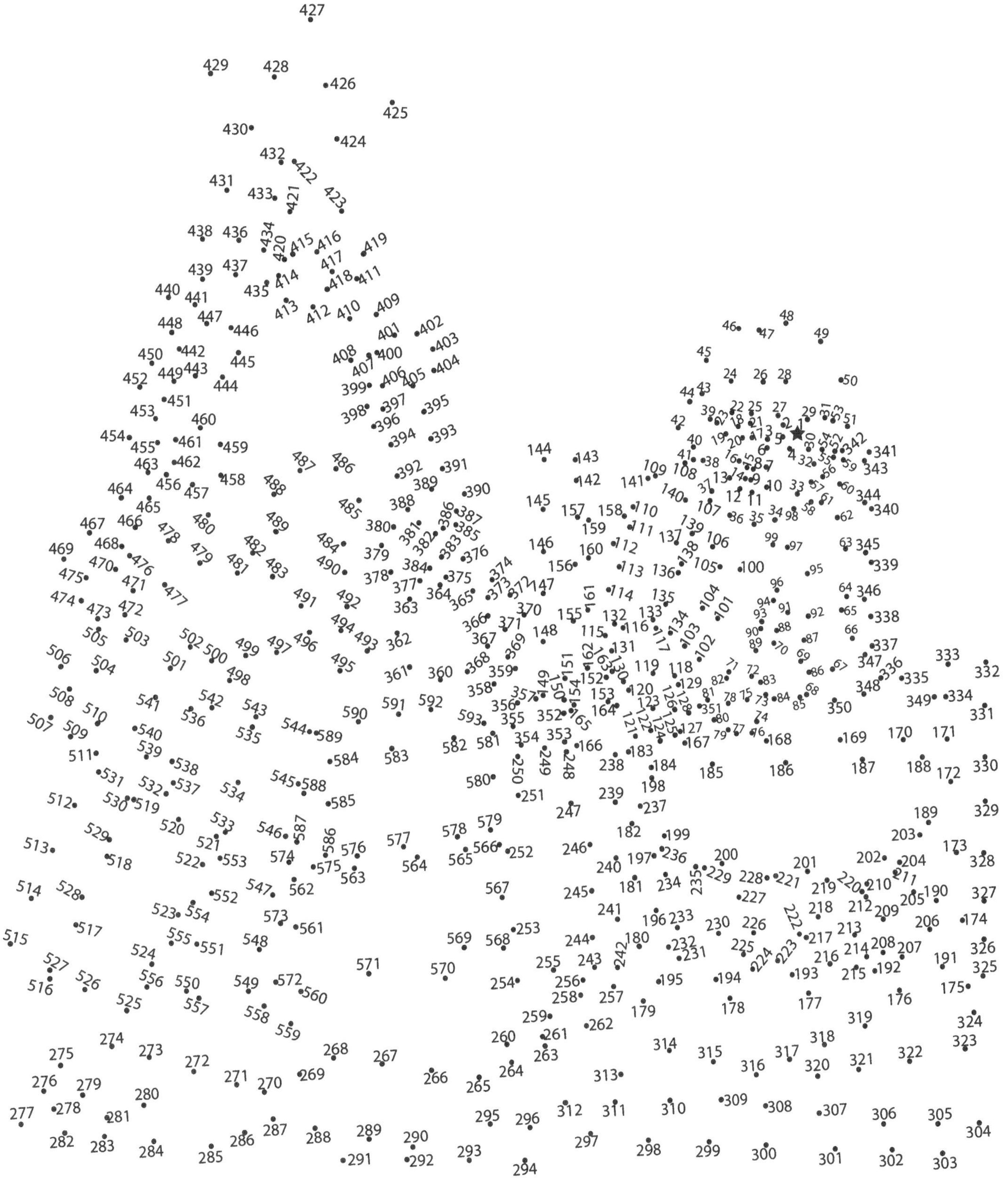

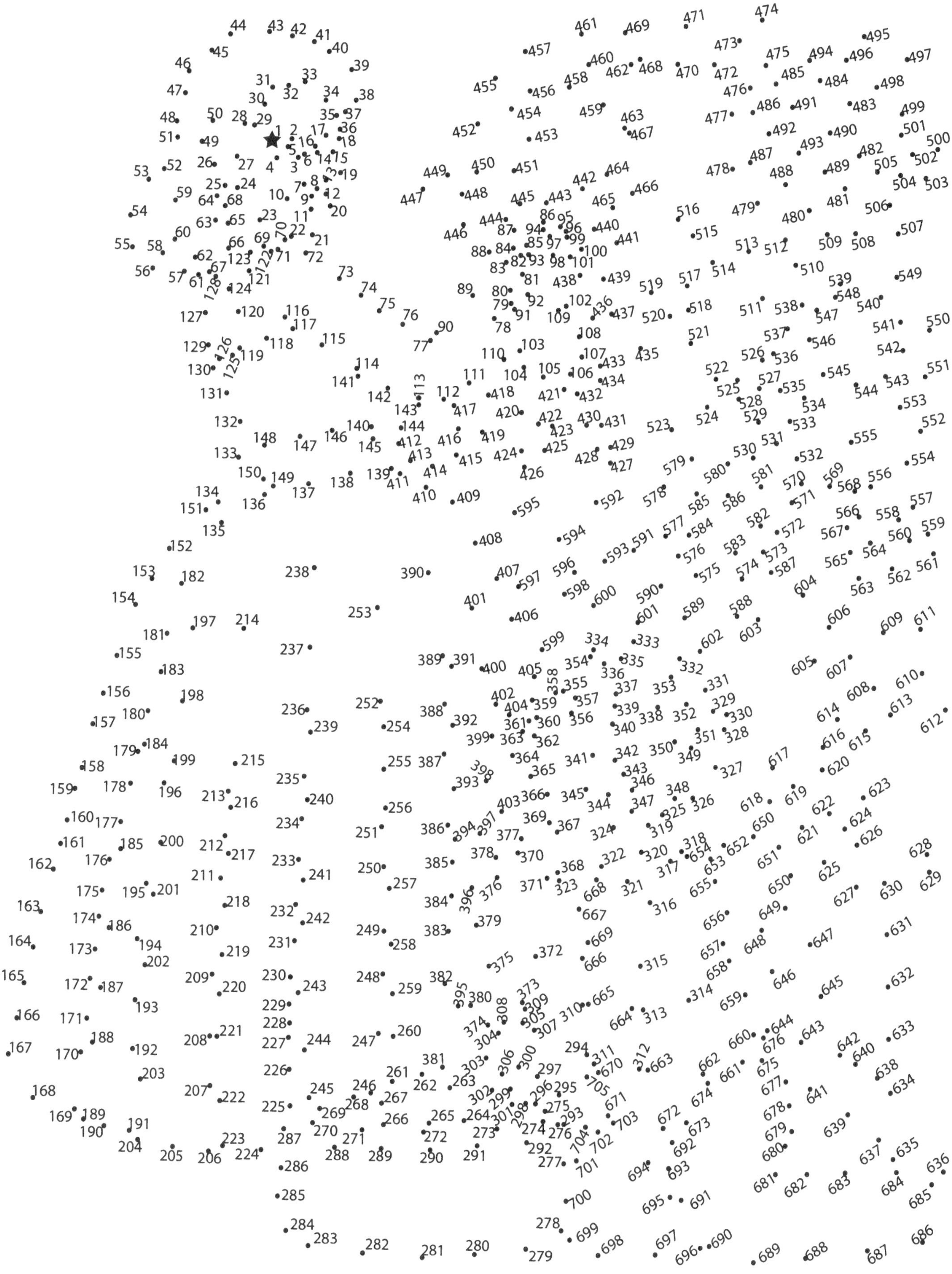

*Enjoy a couple of bonus
images from our other
Dot-to-Dot Books*

Find our books on Amazon.

Large Print Dot-to-Dot for Adults
Puzzles from 156-487 Dots

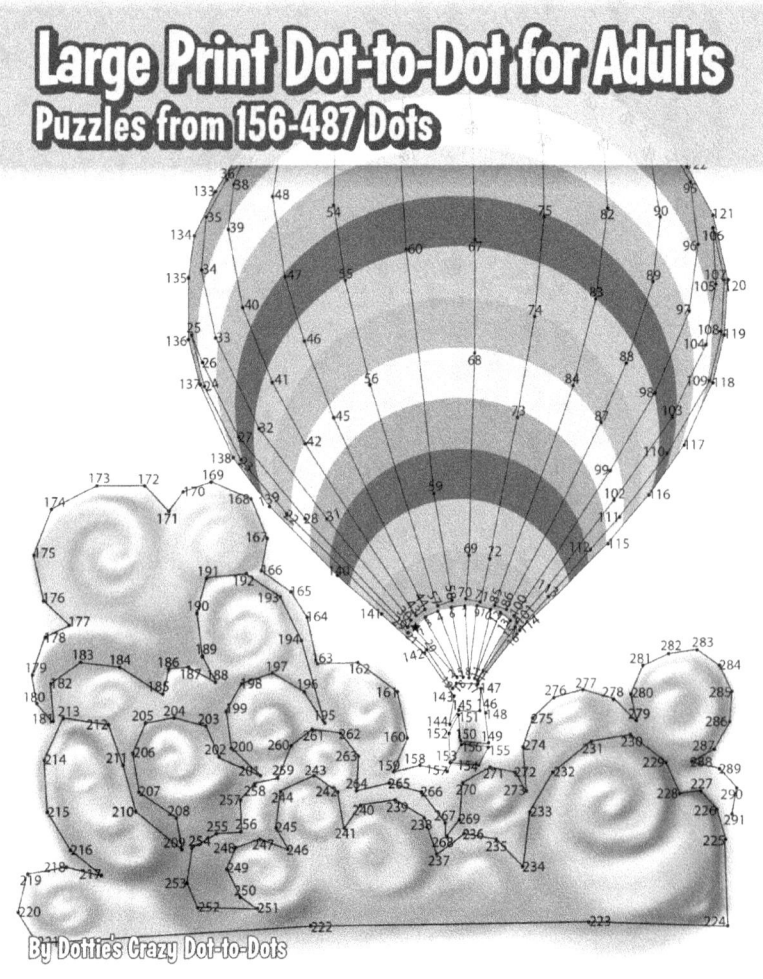

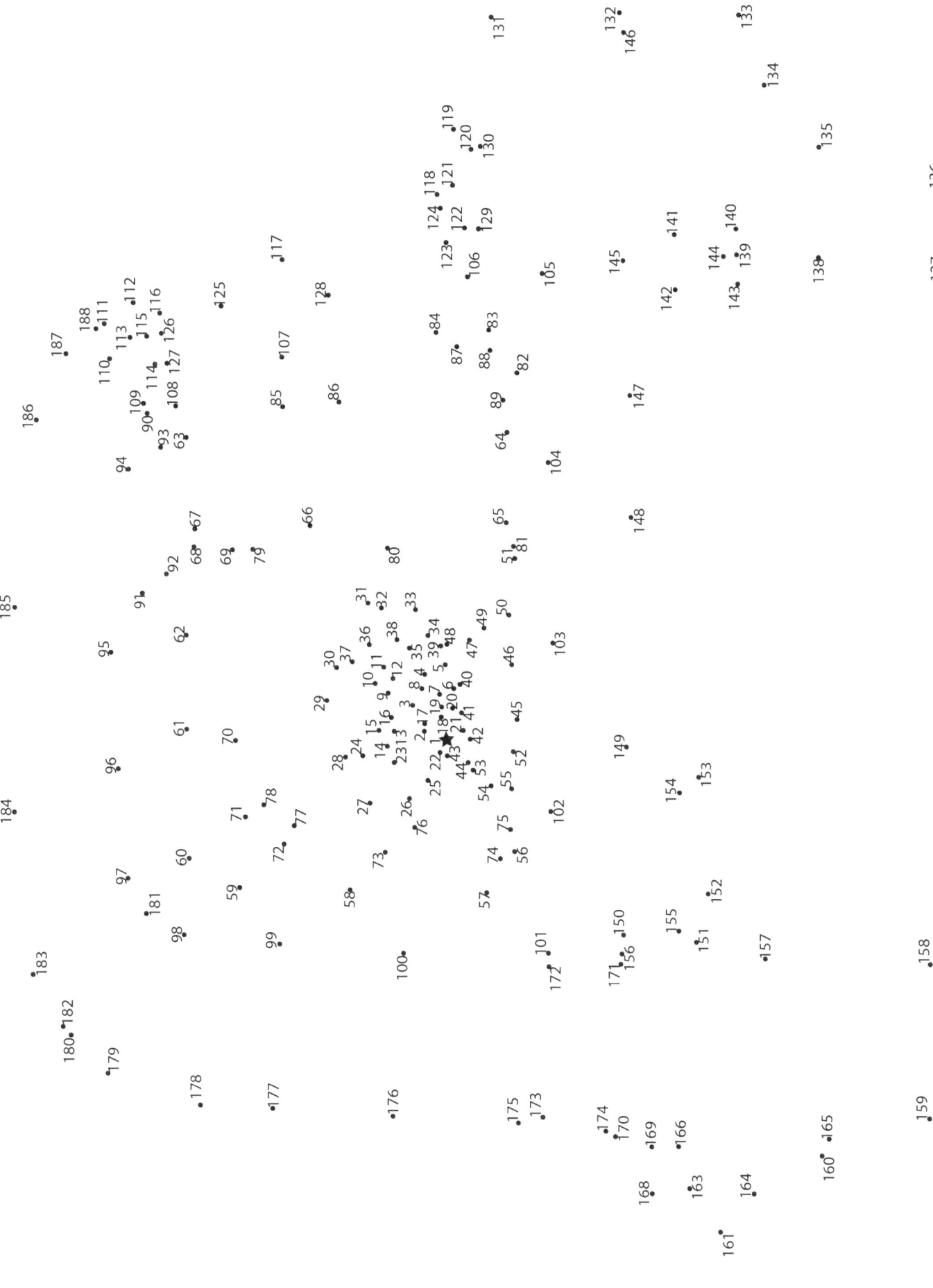

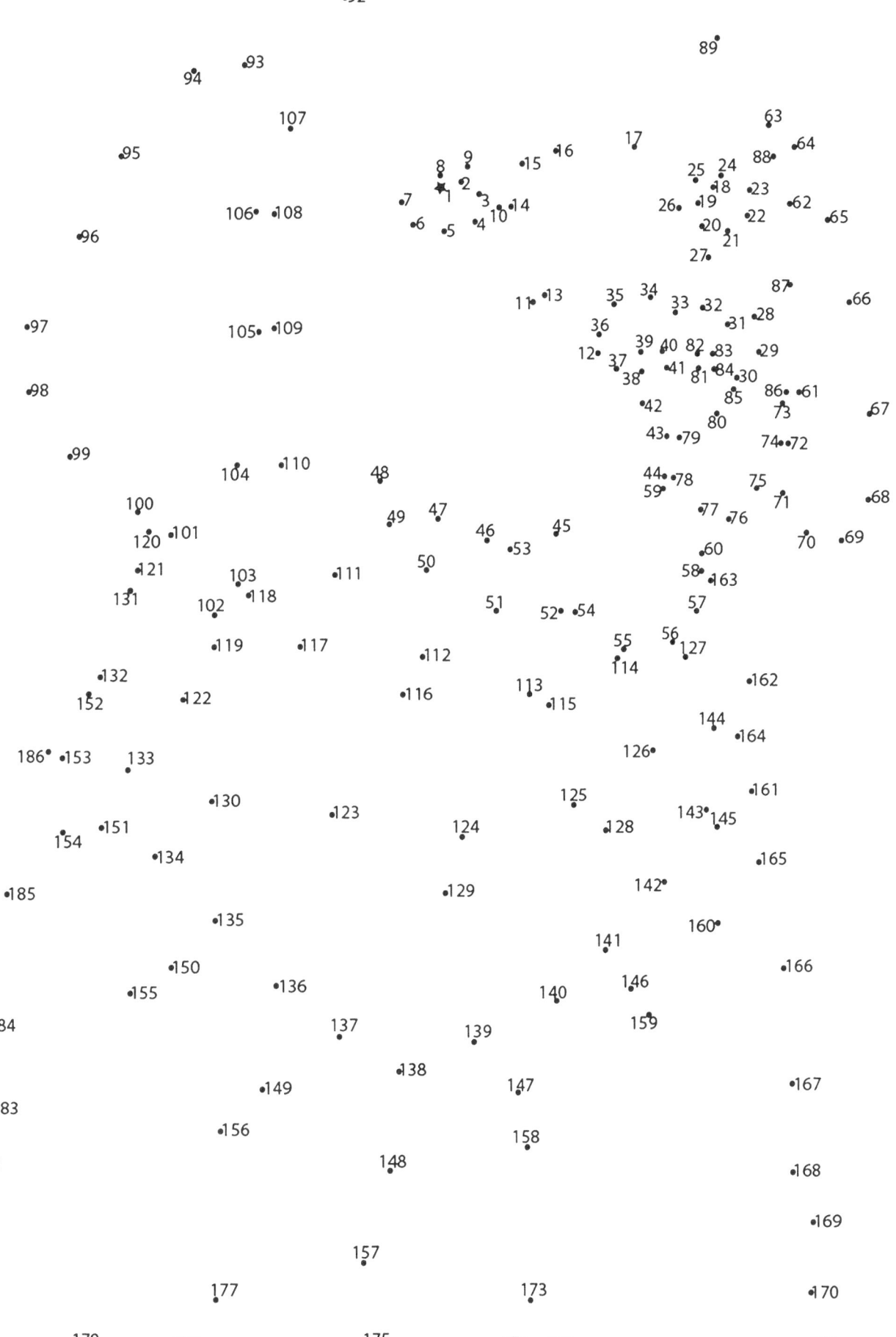

Big Book of Large Print Dot-to-Dot Puzzles
Large Print Puzzles from 156-563

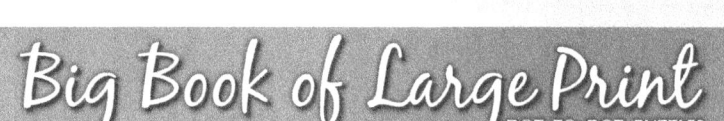

By Dottie's Crazy Dot-to-Dots

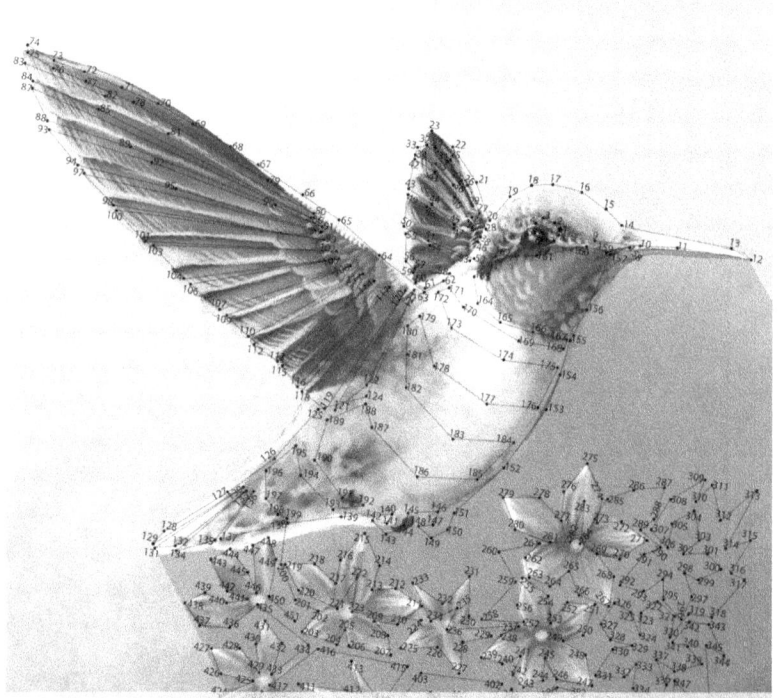

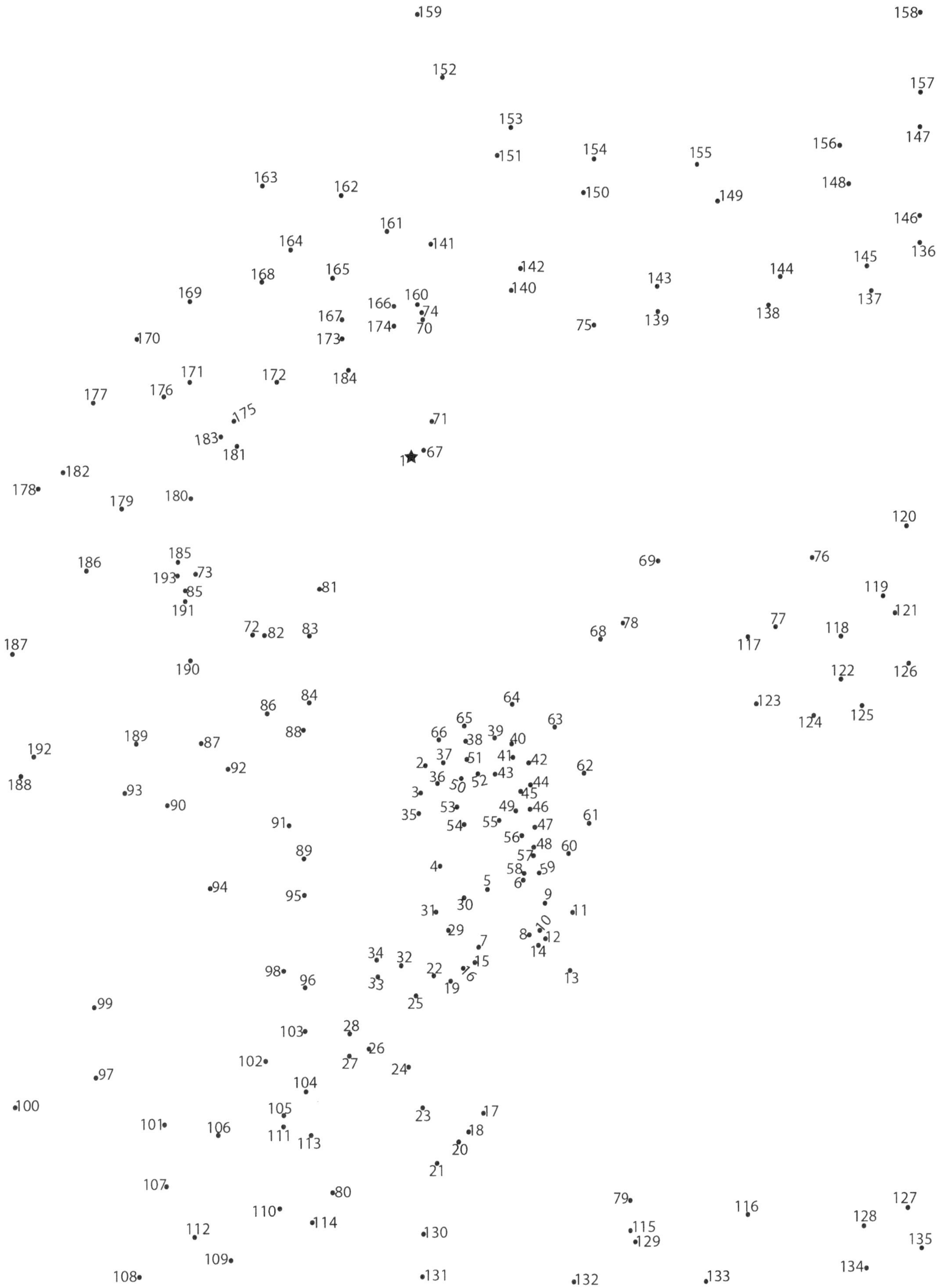

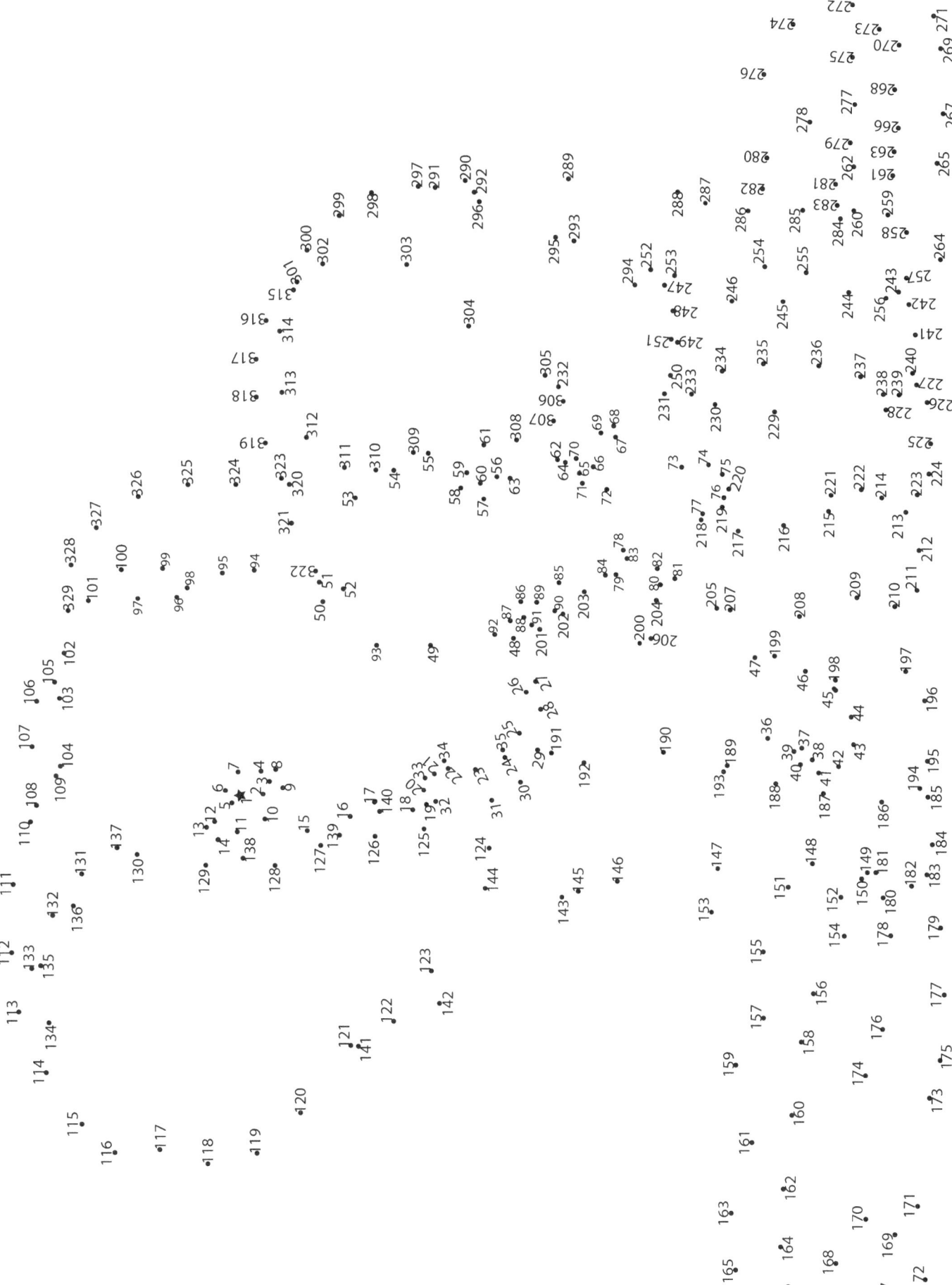

Answer Key

(start from top left to right)

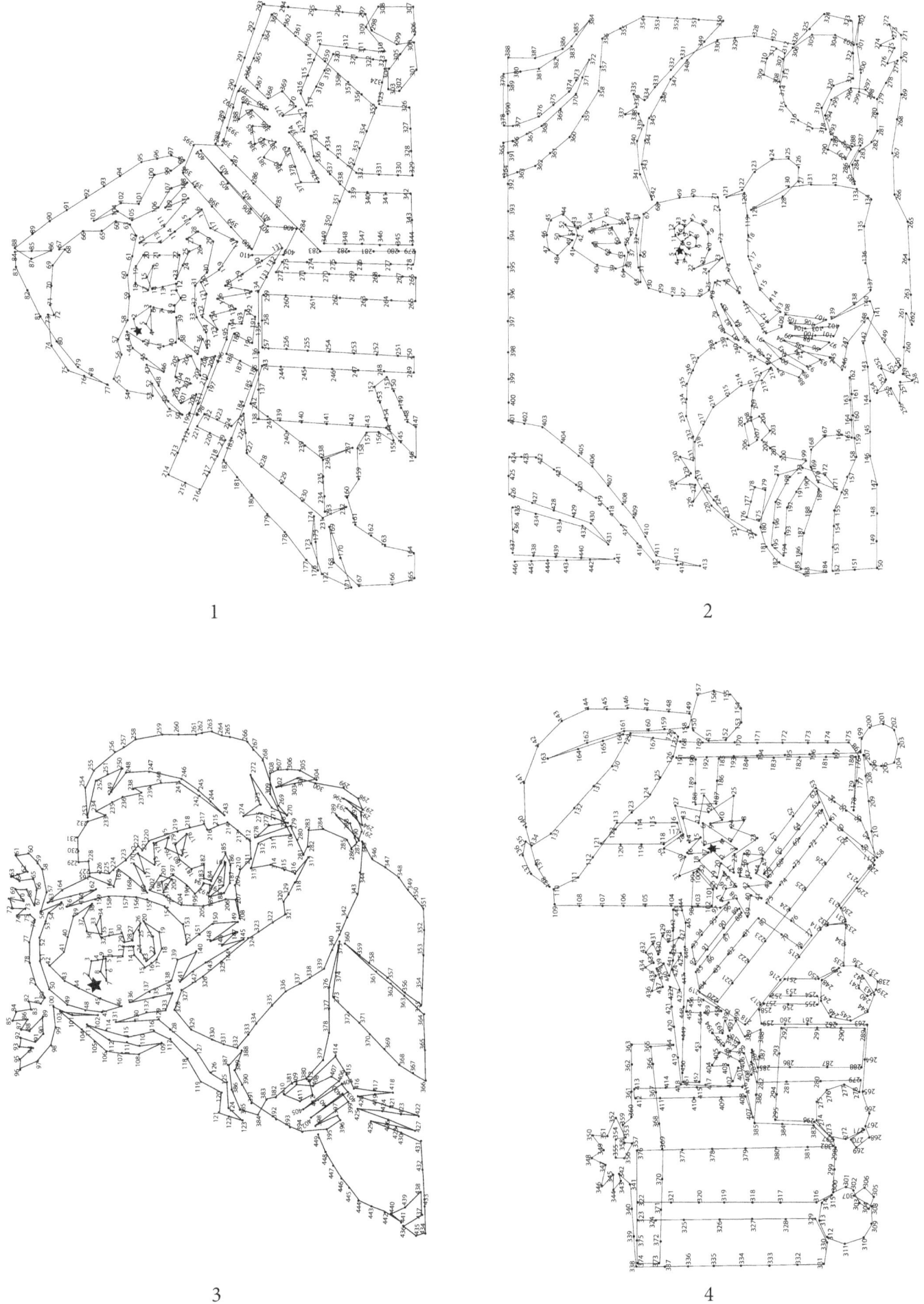

1

2

3

4

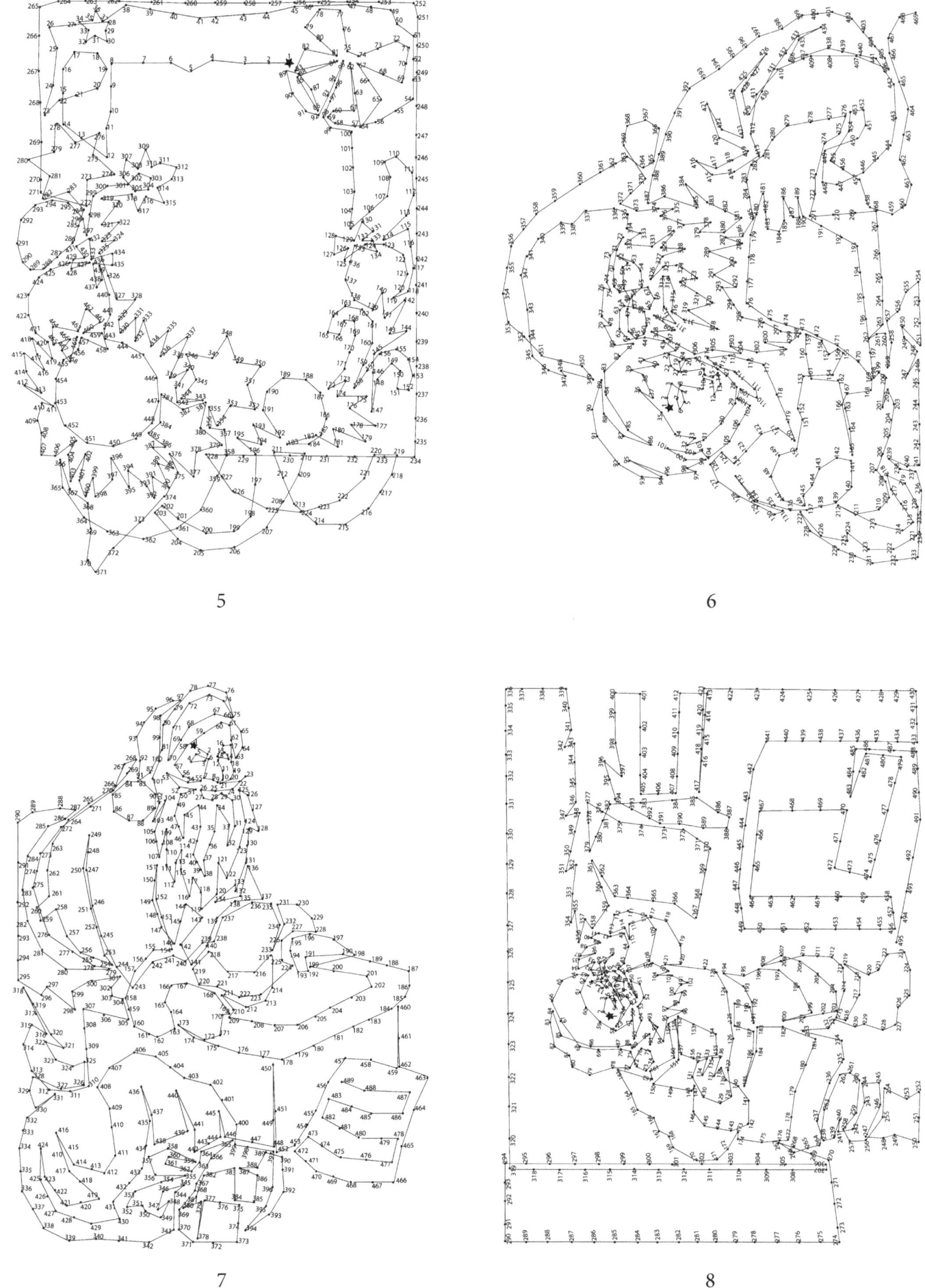

5

6

7

8

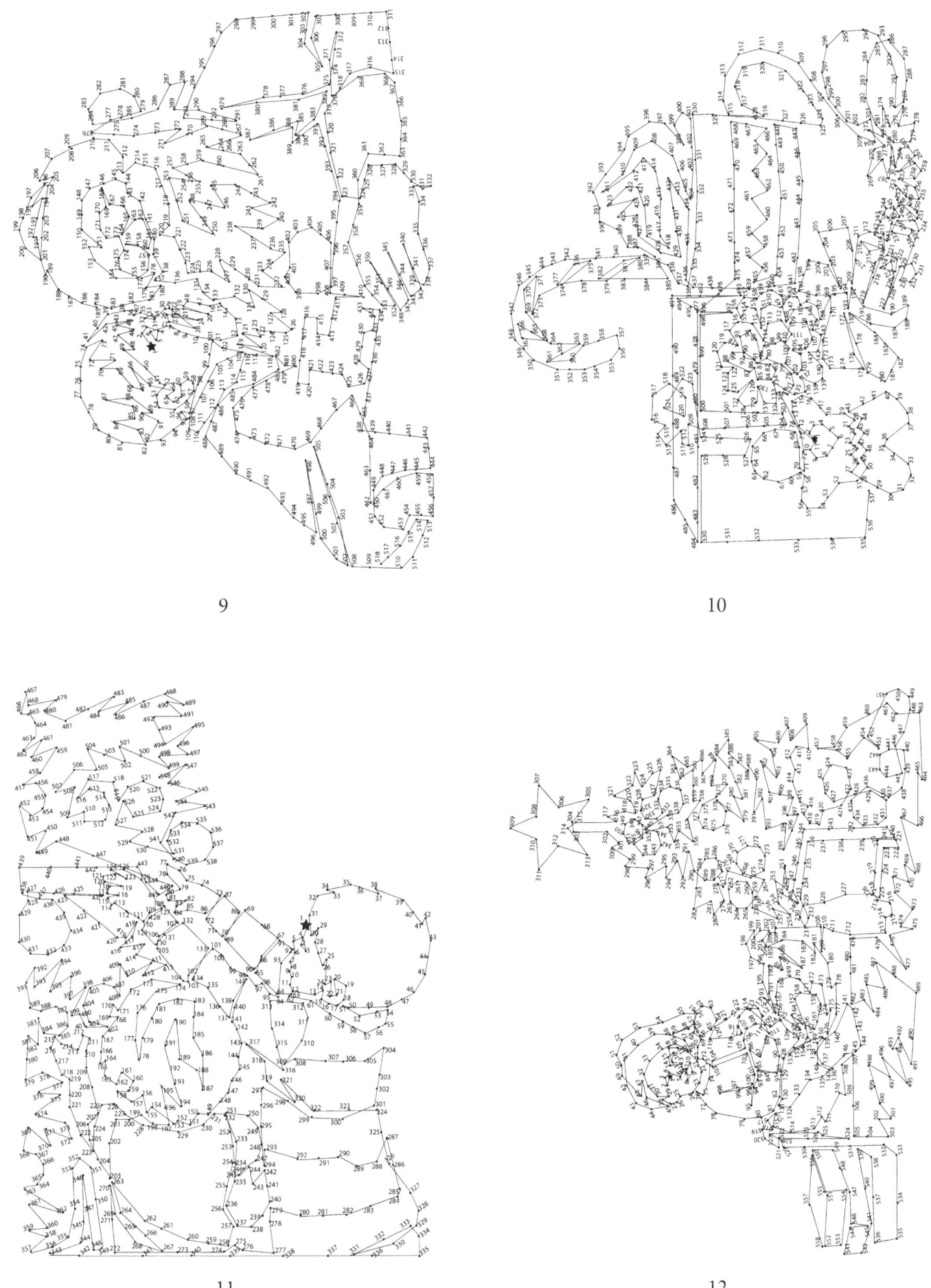

9

10

11

12

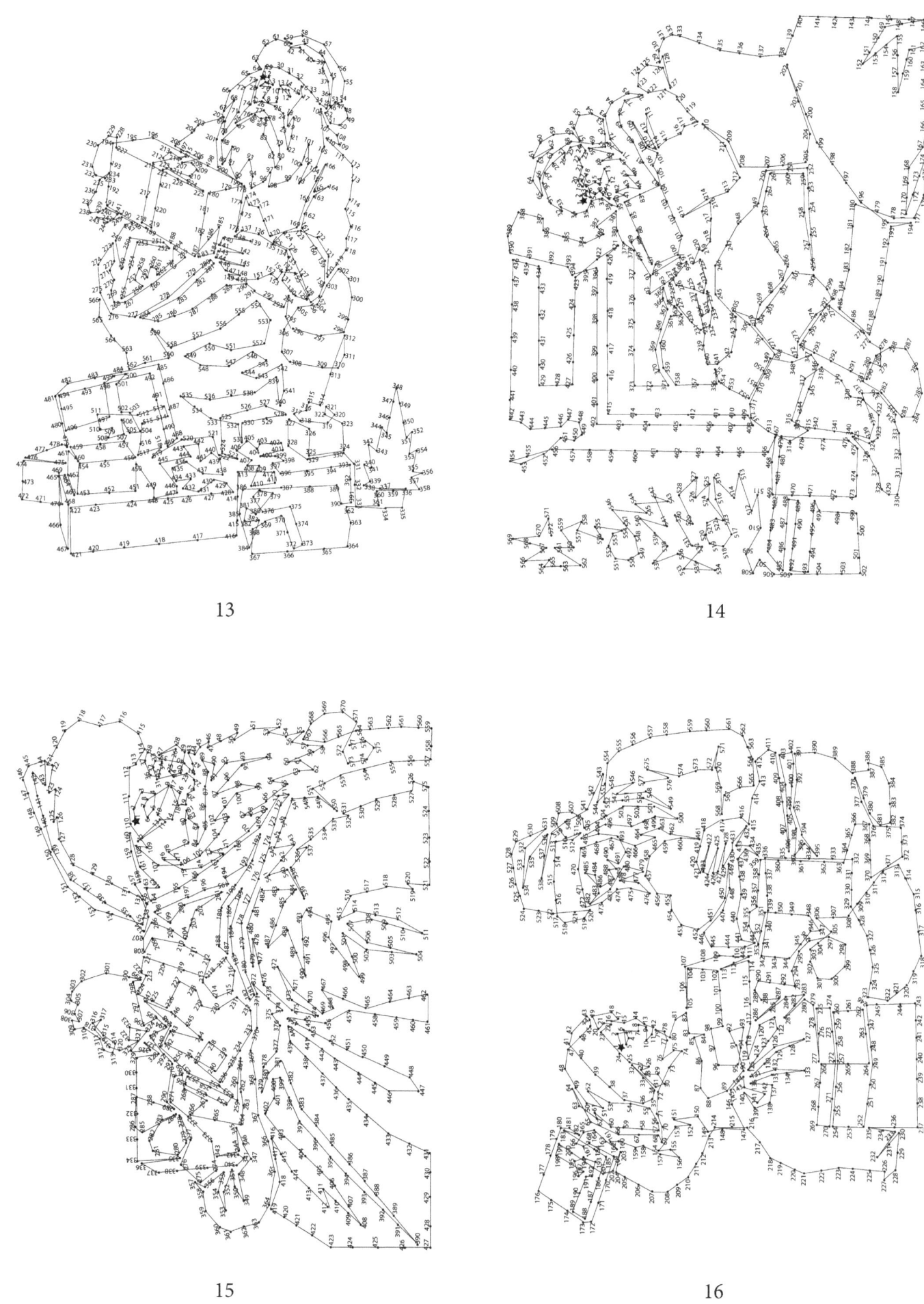

13

14

15

16

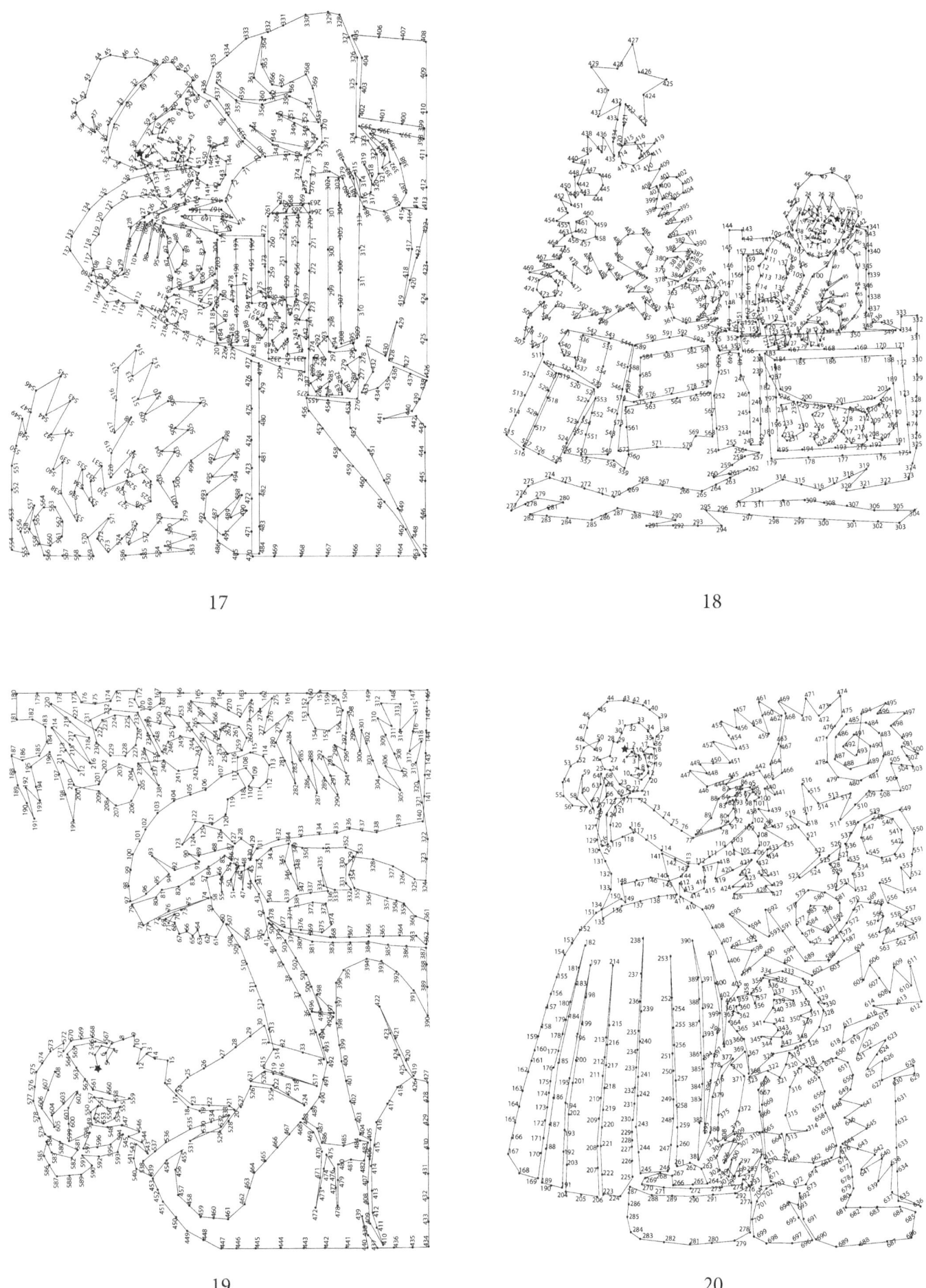

17

18

19

20

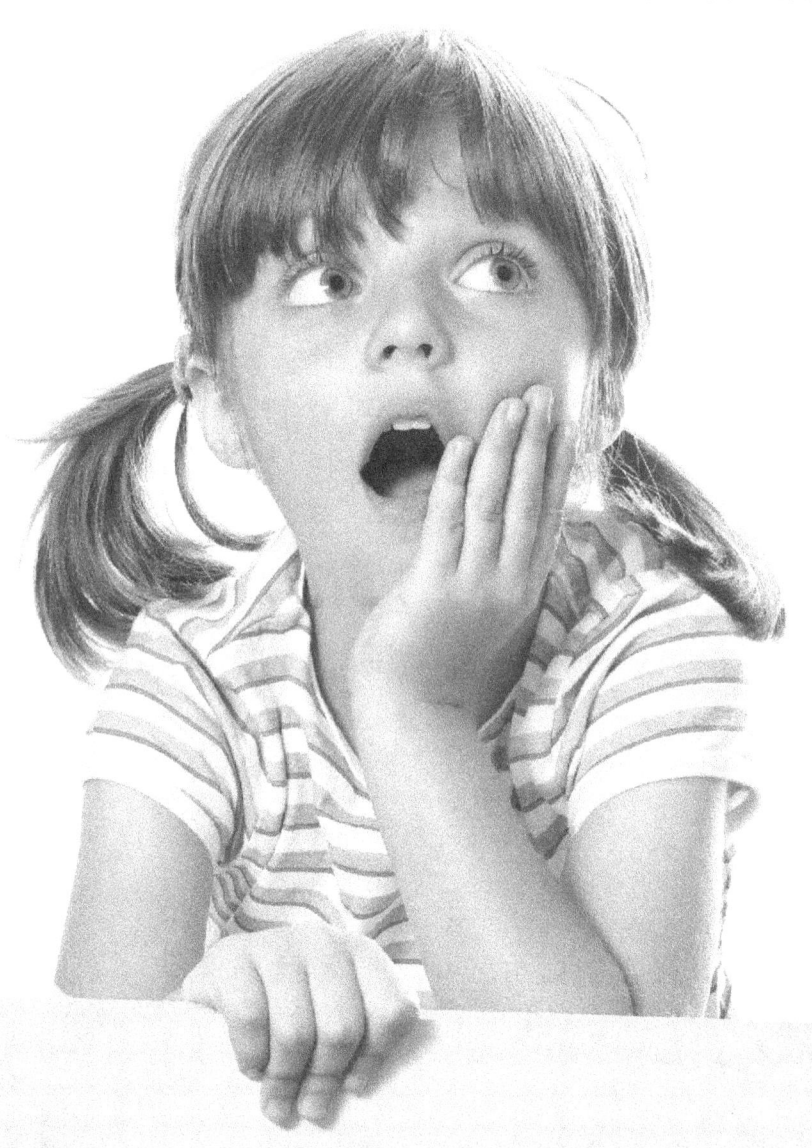

Did you know?
We Have a Great Mailing List!

Free Downloadable Dot to Dot Pages
Monthly Giveaways
Exclusive Discounts
& More!

 SCAN ME

Scan the QR Code with your phone's camera
or visit DotToDotClub.com to Join

thank you

for your purchase!
If you enjoyed this book,
please leave a review. As a
very small independent
book publisher, every
review helps us compete
with larger companies.

scan me

Scan the QR Code
to Leave a Review

(open your phone's camera
and hold it up to the
square)